AM I STILL

A SISTER?

How come the tears come sometimes? How come my throat hurts and I feel sad? I thought only happy memories lived forever.

ORDERING INFORMATION

Send $5.00 plus $2.00 shipping and handling to:

Big A & Company
106 Constellation
Slidell, Louisiana 70458

ISBN: 0-9618995-0-6

Library of Congress Catalog Card Number 87-71613

Copyright© 1986 Alicia M. Sims

Printed by Starline Printing, Inc.

ACKNOWLEDGEMENTS

A special thanks and a BIG HUG to my terrific friend and illustrator, Jim Maus and to my Mom and Dad, Darcie and Tony Sims. They listened, typed, drew, and read. Most of all, they cared.

And thanks, BIG A, for teaching me about LOVE!

You ALL have a special place in my heart.

Love,

Alicia

I've known Alicia all her life and from the beginning, I knew she was special. She added a sparkle to our marriage that convinced us to add another child to the back seat of the station wagon. When our son, Austin, was born, the family was complete and we set about being happy. But that was not to be and Austin Van Sims died just after his first birthday from a rare form of brain cancer.

We fought for Austin's life with a nationwide search for answers that forced us to send Alicia to live with my sister and brother-in-law. When we were finally able to reassemble the family, we were faced with the destructive forces of cancer. We took our son home and tried to rebuild a family. We all learned to care for Austin in his last months and Alicia grew expert in providing the tender touch of a big sister. She taught him to sit up, to play patty-cake and to pull the string on a music box. He taught her how to love without condition and how to die. We all learned you can't paint a rainbow on the wall and think it's going to stay. In the end, we couldn't catch it and we had to let the rainbow go.

We called Austin the Rainbow Man and we call Alicia our Sunshine because she came peeking back out behind the dark clouds of grief and reminded us of the continuance of life. She forced us to get up every day and chided us into smiling again.

She got an early and unintentional education in death, but she taught us the path of survival. These thoughts she shared with me were her gift . . . and with her permission, I share them with you. They are testimony to the strength of childhood and the beauty of sisterly love. They are treasures from a special child.

With love,
Alicia's mom

Dedication:

To My Mom and Dad,

Who gave me a pad and a pencil and believed in me.

My name is Alicia. I am 11 years old and in the 7th grade. My brother, Austin, died of brain cancer when I was four. He was 13 months old and I loved him more than anything. I loved being a big sister and taking care of him.

We called him "Big A" because he was so small, but he fought so hard to live, he must have been part giant. I used to hold him and snuggle with him in Mom's big rocking chair and Austin *always* had a smile for me. We "talked" a lot and I shared all my secrets with him.

My brother was so special to us that we called him the Rainbow Man. Even when he was so terribly sick, he smiled for me and it was like a rainbow peeking around the dark clouds. I could always get him to grin and when he smiled, then I wasn't so scared.

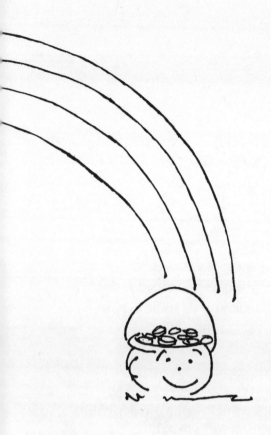

My mom and dad call me their sunshine. We laugh and joke a lot. We did when Austin was alive, too. But right after he died, it was pretty dark for a while. It seemed like we would never be happy again.

When he died, I didn't have anyone to share anything with, so I wrote some letters. Now I want to share them with you because maybe you need to know you're not alone in your sadness. I've been there, too.

I hope you have some memories that make you happy. And I hope you can find a rainbow for you.

Hello Rainbow,

This is Sunshine. How are things in Heaven? I sure miss you, baby brother. It's been a long time since we've been together, but I still remember my rainbow baby.

I've collected a lot of memories of you, Austin. Some are good. Some hurt. But like Mom and Dad said, the sun is coming back out and we're learning to smile again. It hasn't been easy, Big A, but I'm making it.

There are so many things I want to share with you! I've had so many thoughts and feelings about you and when you died. Sometimes I can't talk about them, so I write them down. I guess it's okay to share them, maybe there are other kids who are keeping feelings secret, too. Wish we could all get together and pass our fears around, then I don't think they would be so bad.

Don't worry about me, Big A. Things are getting better down here, too. Hope you're happy.

Hugs and Kisses,
LOVE,

Alicia

I'm supposed to say a Thanksgiving grace today at the table, but I don't feel very thanksgiving . . .

What are we supposed to be thankful for? God took our baby away and we're supposed to still believe in HIM?

The table is set, the turkey smells good and everyone is gathering around . . . everyone that is, except my baby brother. WHY didn't HE let Austin live? WHY didn't HE help him get better so he could grow up with me? I don't want to be alone. I don't want to go to school alone. I want to be a sister. I don't want two turkey legs!

Hey God, I'm talking to you! Can you hear me? WHY don't you answer?????????

Or do you and sometimes I just can't hear? Well, anyway, I guess I'm thankful for the little while Big A was here. We did have fun sometimes.

So, thanks God for that little while.

Hello Austin!

Texas doesn't have any snow and I miss it. Remember when we lived in Michigan and we had LOTS of snow?! It used to take Mom HOURS just to get us ready to go outside and I always had to go to the bathroom right after she put on my mittens! I was so bundled up I couldn't even move and she expected me to play? And you—oh Big A, it makes me laugh to remember how tiny you looked in your snow-suit and 200 blankets! I could hardly even see you under all those covers!

We made a snowman with Daddy once and you looked so happy when Mom held you up to Mr. Snow's face. Dad and I threw snowballs at each other, but we didn't throw any at you—you were too small then. I could hardly wait until you grew up! Then we could go sledding and skating together and make angels in the snow. Boy, we would have fun when you got bigger!

But you never got bigger, Austin. You never got to play in the snow with me. And the next year when it snowed, no one wanted to make angels in the snow with me. Mom tried once but she started crying and her tears left little icy streaks on her face. And then I cried and the snow just got cold and wet. And we didn't play outside much that winter.

And now we've moved to Texas and they don't have snow here so no more snow angels, Big A. But if I did find some snow, I'd make the biggest angel ever and I'd never let it melt!

I'm missing you, little brother. I hope spring comes soon.

Love,
Your BIG sister

Dear Austin,

I wonder if you'll get mad at me if I tell you this. It's been bothering me for a long time. Have you ever heard of magic wishes? Once, when I was little and you were littler, I wished you would go away forever. I sure didn't like you having all the attention. I really didn't like it when I had to go live with my cousins. And it was all because of you.

And then when you did go away forever, I knew I had magic wishes. Those kind of wishes were scary. Once I wished real hard that another kid would get in trouble. And he did! I decided not to make wishes like that anymore.

Once I wished a monster would swallow up the whole world. But I guess my wish wasn't any good because we're still here! I'm glad that wish didn't come true. And I really wish my other two wishes could be undone.

But now I'm older and I know that there aren't any magic wishes. So, I don't feel bad about wishing you were gone. Now I only feel sad. If there were such a thing as magic wishes, I would wish for you to come back forever!

Please don't be mad at me, brother, for wishing such awful thoughts. I was a lot younger then and it hurt me so much to have a sick brother. I didn't know what else to do.

Hugs and Kisses,

Alicia (former wisher)

How come everything comes in two's? Two bicycle wheels, two socks, two cookie halves, two peas in a pod, two clouds in the sky, two shoes, two eyes, two ears, two turkey drumsticks, two EVERYTHING! Except me! There's only one kid in this family now—there used to be two . . .

I used to have to share the back seat. I used to have to share my toys and I always shared my cookies. We shared Dad's wrestling and Mom's lap. I shared my books with you even when we couldn't read. And we shared secrets—
you and me.

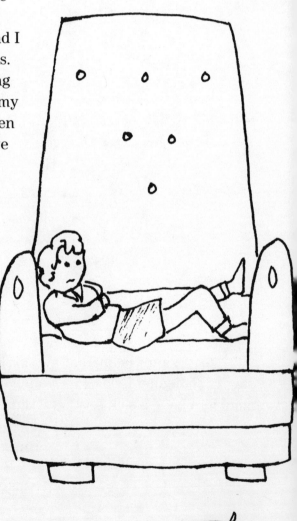

And now I don't have to share anything. I have the whole back seat to myself—two windows. I have whole cookies now, not just a top half. I didn't used to like to share but now I wish I could.

Two. Both. A pair. Together. Double . . . half.

Two of everything except us . . .

A BOOK REPORT
BY
ALICIA M. SIMS

There is an empty space in my life. My brother died. I chose this book because I thought it would be okay to see how other people feel when someone they love dies.

I learned that death is all right for some, but terrible for others. Some think death is a relief from life. Others aren't ready to leave. Some people do not have choices. They die in accidents or suddenly get sick.

When death comes suddenly, families haven't had time to get ready. So they are surprised and very, very sad. Even when we knew my brother was dying, we were still very, very sad. Death brings an empty space. Empty spaces are sad.

Dear Austin,

How are things going in Heaven? How are you doing in school? Is there school up there? Did you get "A's" in school? We had to write a health report and I did pretty good. I wrote a book report, too. I like all my teachers except one.

I have a few boy friends. How many girl friends do you have? I get to play my flute for a whole half hour in front of the class! I'm nervous!!!!!!! Wish you were here to hear my flute solo. Maybe if I play good enough you will hear me.

Love,
A
Flute Soloist

Dear Brother,

I'm so mixed up inside. I don't know what to think anymore. Sometimes I'm really mad at you. You left me! And I really wanted to be a big sister. Sometimes I'm guilty too. I wasn't with you when you left. Maybe I could have saved you.

Then sometimes I want to scream. Maybe that would make the hurt go away. I cry a lot, but mostly inside me. There aren't many tears left on the outside anymore. Sometimes when I'm alone, I wonder about you. I can even see us together sometimes, walking in the woods and talking.

Maybe I'm going crazy, Little brother. Lots of times I get the giggles and can't stop. I'll be thinking of something you did that was funny and all of a sudden, I'm filled with happy memories. Remember when I taught you how to pull the music box string and how surprised you looked when the music started? I still get tickled when I think of that.

But sometimes right in the middle of a good feeling . . . SNAP! And I remember it's just a dream. You're not here anymore.

Sometimes I feel like a whirlwind is inside me and I'm spinning like a top. It hasn't been easy since you died.

Love,

Alicia

Dear Austin,

I got braces yesterday. You should see me! I look like the front fender of our car.

Mom says I look like a teenie bopper. I feel old. Wonder what you would look like in braces?

Braces are a real pain . . . in the mouth! Dad says maybe I won't talk so much now, but I can still think. And I think about you a lot.

Love,
The Tin Grin

TiNSEL
MOUTH

Dear Austin,

Today I was at the park. There were swings and slides and a funny climbing thing that kind of looked like a train. There were picnic tables, grills, and some nice trees, everything a park would need except you. It's early spring and the trees are beginning to bud and the air is sweet and soft. It was a good place to be and I wish you had been there.

I tried out the slide and climbed for awhile on the climbing train. The birds were really loud. They sounded like they were having a good time. It was warm and breezy and when I sat on the swing, I got an idea. I started swinging higher and higher. My legs got tired from pumping so much, but I still went higher. I wanted to touch the clouds with my toes because I knew Heaven wasn't much farther away.

I went higher and higher and the clouds got closer . . . could you see me, brother? Did you hear me laughing and calling? Even the wind seemed to be pushing me and I knew I was close to you.

Then it was suppertime and I had to go home. Mom wanted to know why I had such a special smile when I got home. I just told her I had been talking with the clouds . . .

And she said she had been feeling especially close to you today, too.

Hugs and love,

Alicia

I was riding my bike today after school and it seemed like everybody was in two's. Everybody had somebody else except me. So I rode faster and harder because I wanted to leave that loneliness behind.

But I ran over a rock and fell. Boy, then did I want you there, Big A! I wasn't hurt very much at all, but I wanted somebody to stop and care for me. But the only thing there was that stupid rock. I kicked it away and went home.

I wonder if rocks get lonely too?

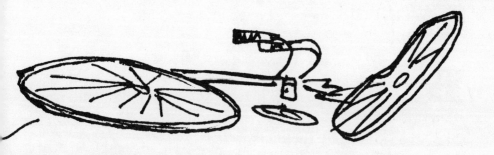

Dear Austin,

I've never told anyone this, but I sure was jealous of you when you were alive. I almost hated you sometimes. And even now, I'm jealous a little because it seems like Mom and Dad are still doing things for you. Sometimes I feel left out—especially when Mom leaves on business.

I really wanted you to be my baby brother, but you were everybody's. Everybody was always worried about you and how you were doing. Nobody (it seemed) cared much about me. Everything we did was for you. Mom and Dad even sent me to live with Aunt Debbie and Uncle Ron and the boys. I liked being with them, but not for soooooo long. I used to wonder about you and what you were doing and I sure missed Mom and Dad. Sometimes I even wished you hadn't come. I wanted to punch you and Mom and Dad. So, I punched my cousins instead.

I hope it's all right to be jealous sometimes . . . were you ever jealous of me . . . I lived and you didn't.

Being jealous isn't nice. It feels heavy and ugly. But Mom says when you really love someone, then it's okay to share even your ugly thoughts.

Thanks for listening, Big A. I don't feel so ugly anymore.

Hugs and Kisses.
Used-to-be-jealous
Big Sister

Dear God,

Do you have birthday parties in Heaven? Today is my baby brother's birthday . . . will you give him a party today, please?

We only had one birthday with Austin and it wasn't enough. We had paper hats, balloons, presents and chocolate cake. We had a pizza party at Shakey's and Austin even wore a hat. He didn't like the pepperoni, but I did!

He was so skinny but he sure grinned when I gave him a finger full of frosting to lick. He didn't look so sick when he smiled like that. With all our family and friends at the party, I didn't feel so scared that day. Maybe Austin would get better because we had a birthday party for him. I gave him a pull toy because I wanted him to get better and play with me. We could have pulled that toy together like brother and sister are supposed to.

God, now we don't have a cake or candles or presents to wrap for our baby. Will you light a candle for Big A today? He likes chocolate cake and *lots* of frosting and ice cream. I do, too.

Has he grown much? Is his hair still so blond? Does he smile? Oh God, hold him tight. We liked to snuggle.

Will you kiss him for me, please? And say Happy Birthday Austin. I love you, baby brother. I love you.

Dear Brother,

What is your zip code?

> Love,
> Alicia M. Sims   79605

ALICIA

SPECIAL DELIVERY

Hey There Brother,

I have a real boy friend now! Do you have a girl
friend yet?

> In Love,
>
> *Alicia*

Dear Kiddo,

Sometimes I feel so close to you. I can almost feel you hugging me. I wish you were. Sometimes, like now, I can talk to you and if I close my eyes, I can see your grin. And that makes me smile.

I wish we could walk in the woods together. I could show you all the birds and we could maybe climb a tree. We could laugh and chase each other and we'd be happy. Mom says we'd probably argue and I guess she's right, but I really don't believe her!

Sometimes when I am listening to records, I almost hear your voice and I pretend we're sitting together . . . like brother and sister. Do you ever feel close to me?

Love,
Me

Dear Austin,

Today I started class in a new school (again! SIGH). I sure wish Daddy wouldn't move around so much. He doesn't know how hard it is to start all over again every time we move. He doesn't know how to answer the kids when they ask about my brothers and sisters.

I almost hate the questions! I wish, sometimes, that no one would talk to me. But they do and I'm really kind of glad because I don't want to be lonely. But, Austin, I don't know how to answer THE QUESTION . . . am I a sister?

Well? Am I? You're dead and I'm not. Does that leave me single? Am I an "only child"? I am the only kid in the family now . . . but it just doesn't feel right if I say I don't have any brothers or sisters. I do . . . I did. I have you, Austin Van Sims, my brother. Or I did . . . once. I remember holding you tightly and rocking in Mom's big chair. I remember teaching you how to pull your music bird and your grin when the music came out! I remember your little fingers curled around mine and sometimes I pushed you in your swing. You were my brother. I was your sister. We were a family and I wanted so much for you to grow up and be my pal.

I remember how little you looked in the crib and how I loved fixing your covers at night. I liked, most of all, sitting with you and Mom and Dad on the couch—all of us bundled up in the quilt together. I felt safe and warm then. We were a family.

We still sit on the couch under the quilt, Austin. And I still feel safe and warm, but there's a piece of me that's lonely for you by my side. I miss you.

Austin, what do I say to those kids? Am I a sister? Are you still my brother? What do you say to the kids in Heaven? You haven't forgotten me, have you?

As long as I don't forget you, I am still a sister!

Love,
Your Sister

Today I didn't cry. The pages of your scrapbook stayed dry. As I turned the pages you came back to me and we played at the park and I laughed at the ducks. I pushed your stroller down the sidewalk and we giggled at the birds. We had birthday cake and chased fall leaves together. As I turned the pages, you and I lived again . . . we were brother and sister.

I used to be afraid of closing the scrapbook. I thought the memories might fade if I didn't keep them fresh. But I haven't opened your book in a long time and today, when I did, you came back and I didn't cry.

I can't believe it's been so long since you died, Austin. I was only a little girl then. And now, when I look at your pictures, it's like a very long time ago—a whole different lifetime.

I've grown up without you, little brother. You are pictures in the scrapbook, memories in my heart and music in my flute. You are a part of me and I don't need the scrapbook to remember you. Maybe that's why there aren't many tears any more. I didn't lose you, baby brother. You really *are* a part of me!

You are the part of love that never goes away.

THE END

ABOUT THE AUTHOR

Alicia Sims was born on Veteran's Day, 1972 in Big Spring, Texas. She grew up in an Air Force family, constantly on the move. When she was three years old, Alicia became a BIG SISTER to Austin Van Sims. Despite his severe and eventually fatal medical problems, Alicia and Austin had a special bond between them. No matter how bad things were, or how much he hurt, Austin always had a smile for his BIG SISTER.

She began writing this book following her brother's death, while searching for answers that no adult seemed to have. She finished the book to help others learn how to survive the death of a sibling.

Alicia is now a teenager, preparing to enter high school. She continues to write and also plays the flute, swims, jogs and enjoys an active "social" life. She occasionally accompanies her mother, Darcie D. Sims, a grief management specialist, on speaking tours and provides insights into a child's perspectives of grief.

She lives with her now civilian family in Albuquerque, New Mexico, where her dad is pursuing a career in health care management.

ABOUT THE ILLUSTRATOR

Jim Maus is a counselor at Nolan High School in Ft. Worth, Texas and a member of the St. Louis Province of Marianists. A native of Illinois, Jim has worked in schools in Milwaukee, St. Louis, and Ft. Worth as a teacher or counselor.

He met the Sims family while he was attending graduate school at St. Mary's University in San Antonio, Texas. He and Alicia's mom were classmates and he frequently visited with the family. Their friendship has continued over the years. Alicia asked Jim to illustrate her book while waiting in line to ride a roller coaster at Six Flags Over Texas. He accepted only after surviving the ride. They both continue to share their love for roller coasters and whenever possible, meet for a ride somewhere in the country.